Song of a Transient and Other Poems

Song of a Transient and Other Poems

Poems by

Benjamin W. Farley

Kelsay Books

Cover design by Shay Culligan

ISBN: 978-1-947465-93-0

Kelsay Books
Aldrich Press
www.kelsaybooks.com

Dedicated to Alice Anne

Acknowledgements

The poems "To the Patter of Rain," "Silhouettes," "The Cinder Road," "Broken Shells," and "Winter Glow" first appeared in the regional journal *Nostalgia* of Orangeburg, SC in the 1980s; the poems "Lilith," "Doves," and "Of Fathers and Sons" were published in the biweekly journal *The Evening Reader* of Laurens, SC, a publication closed since the late 1990s. The author is indebted to both journals for granting all rights to the author, as well as being the first to publish the poems. The author further acknowledges gratitude to the journal *Religious Humanism* for permission to quote "Snow" from its spring issue, 1994.

Readers may be of interest to know that, for the most part, the poems have been grouped in the order in which they were composed, "Song of a Transient" being the first, written in 1958, "Corona Moon" being the latest composed in the fall of 2017. Poems from the first section through "In the Shadowglen" were written prior to 1995, many set in Tidewater Virginia and later around Charlottesville (1958-1971); the remainder were composed while teaching philosophy and religion courses at Erskine College (1973-2000). Between 1995 and 2015, I abandoned poetry to write fiction, returning to poetry only in 2015.

Readers perusing the poems will notice the author's allusion to the "Infinite within," a concept that the author owes to Plato, Augustine, and the philosopher-theologian, Paul Tillich. From their perspective, "God" symbolizes the metaphysical and metaphorical force that grounds human existence. Such references are not intended to infringe on a private conscience's right to pursue one's own quest for meaning and destiny. Rather the phrase acknowledges that we are all part of the mystery of life, of something inescapable, which poetry enables us to celebrate.

One may also note the recurring presence of Nature. Having been reared in the valleys and coves of the Blue Ridge Mountains of Virginia, and later privileged as a youth to hunt and fish across the vast expanses of woodlands and lake country of Fort Custer, Michigan, it is not surprising that my first choice of vocation was forestry with the dream of becoming a forester. It was only midway through college that I was drawn beyond that appeal to consider a different career, succumbing eventually to the call of academia. Any reader, however, who has ever been reared in or around mountains, or blessed to wander their craggy, lofty meadows, or hike their shadowed trails, or fortunate enough to grow up on a rustic tobacco or cattle farm, shorn of the amenities of modern necessities, will understand the appeal of a bucolic life. We all need that sacred place that reunites us with our roots and with ourselves, whether by the sea, or in some high or rolling mountain range, or wherever the Infinite speaks to us. It can be in a park, in an armchair by oneself, or in the hidden chapel of one's soul. There the glory and song of life comes to us, to cheer and comfort us, as well as challenge and probe the mystery of our being. In the final analysis, poetry is a form of prayer, a soliloquy, a lament as well as a hymn of thanksgiving for the mystery of life, along with its power to keep us human as individuals and neighbors.

In addition to the poems in this volume, an earlier collection was published as addenda in *Son of the Morning Sky*, under the title: "Poems of the Knobs," released by The University Press of America, 1996. None of its poems is included in this volume, nor does the present work contain all of the author's poems.

Finally, I wish to express my appreciation to Professor Alexander Ogden of the University of South Carolina and the poet Alexa Selph of Atlanta for their gracious comments, included on the back cover of this work. Above all, I am grateful to my wife, Alice Anne, for inspiring so many of the poems published in this volume.

Contents

Apparitions

In the Shadowglen

Orion

Art and Verse

About the Author

Song of a Transient

Song of a Transient

I've cut hemlock and laurel
And dug in leather soil
I've driven trucks in grain-brown fields
By briar locust trees
I've portered water pipe
Over wet asparagus fern
And boxed warm oily cans of peas.

I've slept on slick cardboard
Under bark-white sycamores
And seen wheat lie down in rain
Strung from black soft clouds.

The End of Summer

And did the evenings linger
Like a Renoir on the wall
A lonely promenade beside the Seine?

Whose vacant eyes are swimming
At Honfleur and St. Michel?
The walls of Chartres rising in the grain.

The sea at San Sebastian
The lights around the bay
I hear the bell still tolling in Burgos.

The shoeshine tough on crutches
Limping toward us in Madrid
The beggars by the Plaza de Toros.

The ride to Barcelona
Your stay at Monpellier
We drink and bid *adieu et bon voyage*.

I drive to Fontainebleau
Then home to Villemetrie
And hear the courtyard echo *mon bagage*.

Broken Shells

Come while the sun
Still hangs on the seam
That divides the night
From the sea.

Come while the tide
And the flow of the surf
Caress the loins of the sandy earth
That yields herself
To the heaving compassionate sea.

Come while the heart
Of Poseidon's breast
Lies thundering in the spray
And the infinite trembling heavens approve
In the blushing smile
Of the evening moon
And I'll fill your hands
With broken shells.

Richmond on the James

1964

Faces of despair
Stare from apartments in the ghetto.
New buildings rise
To erase and hide entire blocks of poverty.
They ring the capitol in a concrete vice.
Jefferson's columns are no longer visible.
To the North and northwest
Lee's Lieutenants ride down nostalgic boulevards
Still guarding the perimeter of the city.
Tobacco market of the world.
Pit-stop North and South.
American. Confederate.
Urban. Forever rural.

The Cinder Road

The moon was lying in a gloom
Of warm ethereal evening amber gray,
And leaf-lorn trees loomed heavily
In porous tissue haze.
Five walking in an evanescent flow,
Our voices on the cinder road too soon
Returning from the pale evasive gloom
To haunt us in the dimly yellow glow.

Orestes Emasculated

Hail, Argos' neurotic scion!
Piteous slayer of Clytemnestra.
Viewing your own mother's breasts did not stay you.
Your father's blood had to be avenged.
What would Freud have judged?
Fromm saw Oedipus in reverse.
Better to slay mother
Than be cursed by sickly powerlessness.
You came close enough to incest as it was,
Embracing Electra.
Misogynist. You and Pylades
Feigned raped Helen with your flesh-hot swords,
Thrusting promiscuous blows toward Ilium's whore.
How the eunuchs fled!
What a sodomistic beginning for a boy
Whose home since childhood had been abused
By Clytemnestra's rule.
If only Agamemnon had lived.

The Sound of Troy Crashes in my Ears

Oh, to rest the jawbone with a smile!
To glance across the aisles of the mind
And find contentment, peace, and bliss.
To reminisce.
To ruminate among the photos of the soul
And find a glimpse
Of time past,
Of time to come,
Of time to be.
And drinking from the cup of hope
Take up again the shield and spear.
The sound of Troy crashes in my ears.
Achilles, Hector, Odysseus,
I come!

Oak Leaves on the Lawn

The leaves are brittle, dry and brown
Like rusted pails in broken mounds
Of flaky rotting metal,
Or beggars in frayed army coats,
Abandoned, wizened, without hope
Tramping lonely into town.

The Colonnaded Boulevard

Confederate Avenue

I walked along
A colonnaded boulevard
Of gnarled elms
That rubbed their hands
Against a cold November sky
That stooped
Like old arthritic men
Staring through thick
Uncombed aching hair
Waiting everlastingly to die.

To Carlyle Marney

El Greco gaped in silence
With jaw-wide glazened eyes
With Velasquez and Bacchus
And Goya in disguise.

The *Guernica* leaned forward
His nostrils pregnant red
While Dali hung the canvas
Of the cup and broken bread.

Bartok for Shostakovich
Played a humble peasant dance
Telling more about our century
Than the curia could advance.

Where Paul Sartre saw no exit
Unamuno found a pass
Pasternak in lonely exile
Traced a footprint in the grass.

Down the steppe a pilgrim wanders
Driven by Valhallan notes
Toward the shadows of a Jabbok
Where the Nameless haunts the slopes.

Silhouettes

For Margaret

I hold our silhouettes in hand
Scissored for us when we were young
By an artist at the Tuileries
When you were pregnant with our son.

Near penniless and dressed in rags
We daily made our promenade
To Notre Dame
To see the windows in the glow of winter sun.

How you laughed at me
The time I went inside that musty shop
On Saint Germain
To ask how much a tapestry would cost
That dated from the fifteenth century!
We were so game for anything.

I remember how that afternoon
When we returned across the Seine
You fainted by the cinema
Because the *petite fonctionnaire*
Who ran the ticket booth
Insisted in was "*Interdict!*"
For you to rest beside the stairs.

We had simply strolled too far
Though you never once complained.

I bought you that Tunisian bun.
You ate it trembling as we walked
Back slowly toward the *pension*.

Now that son you bore is grown
And has a younger brother.
Would that we could take them to
That narrow rue
Opposite the Luxembourg
Where we hid that winter in disguise
As students and as lovers
And visit once again the Louvre,
Napoleon's Tomb, Etoile,
The Eiffel Tower,

And on our way back to some *pension*
Stop by the sandy aisles of the Tuileries
For silhouettes.

Quelle

Comely, faithful, water maid
With household jugs on slender waist
And flowing waves of golden braids,
You turn your handsome face to gaze
Upon a weathered basin
Where pigeons wait in emerald glaze
To drink of your libation.

Stately, silent, plaster girl,
Shapely statuette of grace,
Since my earliest childhood days
You have always filled my thoughts
With reveries of home and hearth
Of memories of long ago,
Of faces in a fire's glow,
Of cabin warmth and family.
Quelle, you will always be
The maiden on the pedestal
My heart will ever cherish.

Of Fathers and Sons

Delirious boy, driven by the muse of whim,
Why do you stare at our wine and silver?
You only smile when you hear music in the streets,
Or the rustling of thighs on kimonos.
How I equivocate at the thought that your are leaving
And have made no provision for return.

The Land? The land is nothing.
I would have sold it for you at birth.
But your eyes when we handed you the purse
Glinted like a warlord's.

So here. Youth is eager. Go.
At least you remember to kiss me.
Remember to write your mother
When you put in at Tyre
Or cross the Hellespont near Troy.

If I could live a thousand years
I would be here
And will always love you.

For P.A. Cabell

I say, "Good bye," to you now, old friend.
They have draped your coffin with a flag.
We know you never left the country,
But your son wanted you covered in blue and white stars,
Honored, Spanish-American Veteran,
Though you didn't want him to.

I could never say this to you
While making visitations,
But I admired you
For the quiet way you accepted every hour.

Soon we will be burying you.
I will read from the 90th Psalm.

Your Mason friends are prepared.
I will never know why you wanted them
But I am glad they are here. For you.

Gertrude and the family have arrived.
Baird came all the way from Savannah.
Jimmy did not embalm you.
It is just as you asked.
Ninety years was a long time to live,
Immobilized to stare at the ceiling.
I think I understand why you wanted to die,
Why you asked me to hand you the pistol
That lay in your drawer nearby.
You cried when I said, "No. I can't do that."
Then you smiled and went on living to the end.

Lilith

I wake, startled, all is dark.
Eve sleeps serenely beside me,
Oblivious to the night's song.
You have come to the window.
I see your breath, your breasts against the panes.
The boughs of the cedar whisper
With trembling voice.
Kneeling, I press my lips
Hungrily to your mouth
Pale in Perseus' glow,
Until the boughs rub jealously along the eaves
And you are gone,
Withdrawn from Paradise's walls.

Anthems

Lincoln

I think of Whitman's poems when I think of you,
Of prairies and log cabins on the Ohio,
Of split-rail fences and corn-rich soil,
Of barefoot boys growing tall into manhood
With muscles hard as ax handles and plows.

I think of your debates with Stephen Douglas,
Of your love for the Union and generals who ill-served you.
Of that national sorrow and battlefield horror
That you transformed and hallowed in a Gettysburg graveyard.

And I think of Booth, too,
And your great bowed head
Where you gaze ex cathedra
From the columns of your Memorial
Across the Potomac into the soul of America.

You have become immortal
And the standard by which we measure ourselves
And all our Presidents by you.

Iron Crosses

Iron crosses,
Always the iron crosses
Held up by iron pins
Angled by old graves.

Ten, twenty, thirty,
Thirty or more iron crosses.
I pass them every evening
On my homeward way.

It's hard to ignore
That many iron crosses,
Hard to forget
What they solemnize.

One could answer Dixie,
Its legendary Rebels,
Or its battle flag
Of red and blue-white stars.

But they signify far more than Dixie,
They symbolize America
And Mr. Lincoln's resolve
That our Union shall be saved.

And so I count the iron crosses,
So many iron crosses,
And pause beside the nearest
To recite:

"Of the people, by the people, for the people,"
On my homeward way.

Epic George Washington

I

Where sunlight drifts on veils of forest vine
Bark-white and bright in dense Virginia woods
O'er brackish leas and sweltering humid swamps
On clammy summer treks up mountain streams
To pause beside a geodetic stone
Beneath a vaulted gorge one afternoon
I see the young surveyor mark his path
And dream of valleys far beyond the Appalachians.

II

He hears the roaring roll of thundering flintlocks.
He sees the choking flash of sulfurous flumes rise thick
And lodge like arrow lances in tight tree limbs
Where hides the stealthy foe from Braddock's men
And darts to drag aside the dying leader
From savage, ravage, and a sad retreat.

III

Whose blood-print foot stains etch the smoke gray snow
By lodgments leaning into bitter winds
Where hungry, freezing, ragged rebel men
Cower over fires low and cold
Awaiting thaws of spring to usher in
The stirrings of campaigns and war again?
Cloaked against the numbing winter night
A general tramps the dark and quiet camps
And dreams of parlors far beyond the Valley Forge
Of wife and home and leisurely Mt. Vernon.

Enough of cold and raw-boned deprivation.
He whispers for the oars to break the silence
And sets his chin for glowing Hessian fires
That hug the Christmas dark across the ice.

IV

Farewell to comrades, troops, and arms
To cannons hauled by ox and mule
To bayonets and mud and meager rations
That keep an army taut and tough and lean.
'T is time for soldering to cease
And time that civilizing arts and peace resume.

V

He paces in the passageways of halls
His presidential powers are so few.
He loves the tiny nation he has followed
From his youthful days of wandering Virginia's forests
To the mantle of old age and statesman prowess.
He sits beside the glow of evening hearths
And stares into the future and the past
And smokes his pipe and quarrels with the logs
That sing and pop and hiss and dance with fire.

Hail to the Chief

'T is well our nation honors you
For years of peace and newfound pride
Though years of fear and mourning, too.

For there are hangars
Filled with coffins,
Flag-draped and guarded
By Marine lance corporals.
And you are there, passing in review,
Solemn in your black overcoat and silver scarf,
Always handsome and determined that our path is true,
But saddened by the exacted cost.

And then abound the images of terror:
Bomb-ripped buildings in Beirut,
Pistols held to pilots' temples,
Bloodstained corridors in Rome and Vienna,
And mourners huddled silently in rows
While Army bands play martial rounds of hymns,
Leaving us in tears and sorrow.

Yours have not been easy years
To oversee or champion.

There may well be more *Achille Lauros*
And crumpled bodies in Gander snows
And interviews on evening news
With future Christa McAuliffes.

But these you balanced with your boldness in Grenada
And your swift avengers
Launched off floating flight decks

From the *Coral Sea* and *Saratog*a.

And far beyond your eloquence in sorrow
Have been your forward-looking calls
Of faith in ourselves and in our causes
Propounded in your "State of the Union" heralds.

Like the Roman Emperors of old
You have been both Pontifex Maximus,
Priest of our Republic,
And Caesar of a decade of troubled
And uneasy truce on all frontiers.

Touring Richmond's Battlefields

For John

By a macadam road in a quiet field
A lone cannon guards a hill
Where McClellan's blue and Longstreet's gray
Swung their caissons into view.

Musket ball and cannonade
Raked the cornrows of the South that day
Littering the furrows with shallow graves
Wreathed in smoke and the glow of fires.

I watch you, lithesome and lean, eyes alert,
Heart palpitating to phantom dreams,
Climb the cannon and stare down slope
To where I point with a sweeping arm.

"I don't know where; I don't know when.
Perhaps it was there, in yonder ravine.
But a part of you and a part of me
Lies fallen here that afternoon

"When our family's cousins and fathers fell
Fresh from the home place we love so well
Fresh from the farms of Abingdon
Against this place called Malvern Hill."

Your young lips part, your limbs grow still
As together we stand on Malvern's knoll
And you and I are one in time,
One in thought, and one in soul.

And may it always be this way,

Wherever you go,
My son.

Gettysburg

For Bryan

March, little man,
      With your Yankee-Doodle hat
      And your Daniel Boone gun.
Let the other children envy you.

I lift you up on top the Anvil Rock.
      How empty the thought
      That it might have been you.
To think they actually got this far!

Now, proud across the distant field
      Shimmering in the summer wheat
      Looms Virginia's monument
Granite-white in summer's heat.

No, no, little man,
      Don't aim your gun out there!
      They are why we've come.
We and they are one.

That's right, little man,
      With your tricorn hat
      And your Davey Crockett gun.
That is why we've come.

But the homage in my heart
      Sinks at the dull recurring thought
      That it might have been you,
Little Yankee-Doodle Rebel boy.

Ike

I once saw Ike in a motorcade.
I waved as his limousine swept by
And caught his smile in return.

I've been to the beaches of Normandy.
I've stood on the Pointe du Hoc.
I've driven along to Caen and St. Lo
And wandered through rows of crosses and stars
Above the sands of Arromanches
And listened to gulls cry over the cliffs
Along that lone French coast.

So I stood on the curb
And followed Ike's car
Till it blurred in a wash
Of traffic lights.

Winter Glow

Winter Glow

At dusk the winter sky loomed clear.
The yellow solar disc had set.
And in the west a faint peach glow
Illumined half the imminent night.

I stopped my car
Beside an antebellum house.
Its columned portico rose greenish-gold
In hues cast by
An old magnolia.

And all across the cold horizon
Bristled treetops
Caught in thin stark silhouettes,
Etched against
That iridescence
Of the soft approaching dark.

January 3, 1986

In the shadow of the tent
We huddled cold and shivered

While icy wind
Whipped the limp flag
They tried to fold
With their numb gloved fingers.

Over the Knollkreg Park
The whining cries of rifles crackled
To the click of metal bolts.

And across the rolling ridges rose
A last farewell of Taps,
Faint and low.

And when we walked back numb
Into the sunlight,
You were young again,
And I a child,
As you held my hand
And we walked along
The sidewalks of Tacoma.

Premonitions

Waking at night to persistent sound
Creaking the vents, I ask,
What is it?

Thrashing high in the treetops
Lashing the leaves,
What is it?

In the morning
Gray clouds scud across the horizon
While wind moans the day long
And dark into the evening.

Outside the night
Hisses with wind
Bending cedar boughs
Pelting the restless shoreline of the ego
With gusts and billows.

A branch brushing against a window
Taps a code
Over and over again.

Nothing is permanent
Nothing endures forever
Even the wind must subside
If not tonight, tomorrow.

I listen to
The visitant noise
Incessant, insistent.

In the morning my mother calls,
"It's about your father,"
She begins, her voice both small
And distant.

Snow

Snow brings a silence
A stillness one can feel
Blocking out all human noise.

Standing in the cold of night
One hears only wind on eaves
Clinking against twigs of ice.

It is a welcome sound
If not an eerie echo of primordial time
A cleansing of our homo sapience,

Stripped of culture's encrustations
And our mortal fragmentation
As effervescent as fine snow.

The night hush
Atomizes all my thoughts
And makes me one

With each infinitesimal spark
Of the silent universe
Mirrored in a thousand monads
Suddenly aglow.

Into the February Morning Air

Soon it will be jonquil time.
Last week the first green spears appeared,
Slipping through black muck and soil
Near the base of pecan trees,
Ringed with round woodpecker holes.

Today I count tree score and more
Blades rising upward
Into the February morning air
And sunshine warmth of afternoons
And early evening mists and fog.

I count the weeks to Spring,
Six left as I recall,
And know that jonquil time will soon be here.

Paradox in Winter

Come, warm January sun
And thaw the frozen ground.
Thin brown lawns lie straw-like all around.
Bleak and bonelike,
They glare in the air.
Yet each shadow harbors crystal glades,
Glistening silver-white on limpid blades,
Lacy and refined.
Such sublimity must lie in cold,
Juxtaposed along the sun's bright path,
Like Plato's fine dividing line
Between twain realms of permanence and mutability.
Contrast and unity, opposites in harmony,
Winter you are the bold return
And shadow-side of light,
The numbing echo of a vast infinity
Warmed by the subtlety of a stark and arduous beauty,
Transcending time's long darkness
With beams of starry light.

October

Autumn, you bring the poet in me to the surface.
Breaking up through sprays of leaves
I ride with Proteus your heady seas
Awed by your scarlet waves and yellow weeds.

Like hills diffused in copper light
Before the cloud-pink sky grows dark
You rise in long, smooth, sloping swells
To cascade blue and brown and white.

Autumn, you are like the sea
Bringing in your golden store,
Only to wash out again
When the woodland tides recede.

Of Star Points in the Infinite

I saw the sky a smoky mauve,
As sunset spread its dying flame
And where the disc had paled a grove
Of pines set dark in twilight's frame.

I walked in silence house-ward bound,
A bat on crooked wings took flight,
It angled toward the shadowed ground
And vanished in the crimson night.

I turned to contemplate the scene
Of Nature's night-advancing scheme,
A marvel equal to dusk's net
Of star points in the Infinite.

Locust Leaflets

I sit by my study widow
Watching locust leaflets descend
In a shower of yellow petals
Driven by the wind
In a swirl of golden plummets
Drifting in the wind
And find my own thoughts scattered
By a restlessness within.

Winter Moon

Cold wind has blown against this manse all day.
Its northwest howling woke me in the night.
Rising I brushed aside the curtain's edge
To find the winter moon near full and bright
Luminous above the wooded hills
Vast and shimmering white.

March

March, you are the maverick month
Bringing in both sleet and snow
Just when Spring opens azaleas
Coaxing peach blossoms to glow.

Some winters I have seen you
Freeze jonquils black and bleak
Transforming hyacinths' fragile stalks
Into tall limp and broken streaks.

Forsythia I gave up on long ago.
Only dogwood petals seem to know
How to survive the vernal cold
Along with purple points of periwinkle.

All else your Death Angel kills alike
Whom Nature's Passover elects to strike.

Soliloquies

Halley's Comet

Hail faithful solar transient!
You bold celestial tramp.
We who are earthbound
Sweep the night skies
With our bargain binoculars
And backyard eyes
Searching for your Q-tip glow
Through our K-Mart telescopes.
I see you now,
Tiny, luminous, translucent coal.

My father was nine
When he first saw you.
Now he lies dying at eighty-four.

Strange that we should
Measure our life spans by your fiery ice
Conferring succession from father to son.

I will not be here to see you again
In the twenty-first century
When you return,
But my younger son
In succession may.

I find that odd to contemplate.
In fact, I'm awed.
Like some visitant god
At eschatological interludes
You draw humankind
Into your stellar infinitude
By your eternal and persistent voyage
Into our solar longitude.

My Father's Watch

I guard a part of you
Some talisman of your spirit
Contagious magic one might aver.

But I carry more
Than your genetic force.

My first impulse is one of pride.
Whose eye does not admire
Ornate gold?

Commodity, utility, legacy,
Cradling your gift in my palm
I feel all three.

I close my hand
And feel its warmth.
Your presence still
The greatest gift of all.

On the Value of Percepts

Sometimes when I am too tired to think
Images struggle to take form in my mind
And before I can visualize their luxuriant dimension
They submerge in the murk of sub-conscious prehension
Without so much as the trace of a face
Or form to console a jejune ego.

Kant is avowed to have said
"Concepts without percepts are empty
And percepts without concepts are blind."

I understand his linguistic contention
And if I must choose between bliss or retention
I'd rather have images trouble my mind
Than experience their absence or blissful suspension.

To Boris Pasternak

Colossus walks in the jungle
When you speak.
Grass blows wind over the steppe
And thunders rain.
The geese come home.
The bear is on the prowl
And the deer steps cautiously
Through the spider's wing.

On Putting Out to Sea

For Jack Pitzer

I weigh anchor
While the night laps
To the sound of a distant dawn.

To launch a dream,
To send it drifting
Past the portholes of the self

Till caught up by the winds of hope and will
It sails out
Into the world.

O tiny thought, I launch thee.
Bend thyself to greet the sea.
Slap the waves

With thy bow.
So what if thy masts shudder
And thy decks spill with tumbling sea.

To lie in harbor
Till thy gleaming runners rot
Is not the epitaph

I dream for thee
When I raise this anchor
And whisper: "Go now. Be off."

Silent friend
May wind and tide bear thee
Toward tomorrow's sun-white leas.

On the Theoretics of Poetics

A poem should have cadence
Though it doesn't have to rhyme
And the cadence it possesses
Can be very ill-defined.

It may involve iambics
Or be written in free verse
As the science of aesthetics
Is notoriously diverse.

But according to tradition
It should mirror some erudition
And venturing into philosophics
Touch on transcendental topics.

But for a poem to have import
It must plummet deep inside
And command what is quiescent
As we fain soliloquize.

And in the final measure
It is still a mystery
As to why some verse we treasure
We define as poetry.

On the Metaphysics of Compost

You have come full cycle.
Waving like prayer flags from Buddhist temples
You wafted green and free
In spring and summer breezes
Adorning nimble twigs on towering trees.

Now you are sodden and limp.
Your ebony loins glisten on the tines
As I hurl you out and breeze-ward

Before you fall to earth
To nourish future seasons
Of seeds and myriad births.

You have come full cycle.
In life you were lofty and free
Aesthetic and bright.
In death you are life-giving
Both lowly and contrite.

To encounter the self in the universe
Is metaphysically of note
When the finite is awakened
In the silence life evokes.

Magna est Veritas

Can anything be greater than the truth?
And what truth illuminates the mind
For humankind to recognize the truth
As either true, great, or possibly divine?

And what extended syllogism is
Self-evident to reason?
Or the indubitable residuum
Of a Cartesian rout
That survives a rigorous season
Of intellectual doubt?

Or does its meaning lie
In what the positivist espies
Based on his Principle of Verification
That what cannot be verified
By measurement and eye
Is simply a hoax?

"Not so!" claimed Zerubbabel,
Turning quickly to his host.
"For *magna est veritas et praevalebit*,
Though He who guards that truth
In glory is concealed."
And thus the Persian king
Enlightened by his friend
Replied to his cup bearer:
"With that, I too agree."

Tracing a Satellite's Path at Night

Jet-like the spheroid's tiny speck
Accelerates across the night.
Bright as a drop of molten gold
It orbits past the faint North Star
And slips into the silent dark.

Now I am left alone
Amid the bright celestial coals
Of the universe's glow
Of vast and distant fires.

O rebel specter,
Minuscule point of fleeting light,
How your passing stirs the soul
To ponder space and time and more.

Apparitions

Mary

You lay on your bed alone.
You pressed your hands against your swelling groin.
The child in your womb was set.
Your woolen gown felt limp and wet.

You turned.
The starlight on the ashen hearth
Seeped through the curtain to the North
And in the dim o'er Bethlehem
You saw the Star.

Your pains resumed.
You cried and coughed.
You rolled nauseated on the cloths
And, lying back,
Sweated in the cold.

You gave him birth.
You wrapped him in a soft warm shirt.
You held him to your breasts to nurse,
Your first-born baby boy.

Zechariah

The aging priest knelt wan
Before the altar
Bronze in incense glow
And waited for the emerald smoke to rise
Itself a sacrifice.

He watched the shadows slant against the wall
And heard his own low voice
Monotonous small
And offered it to God, his only prayer.
An apparition rose beside the flame

A mysticum of strange
Soft, spectral light.
With muffled wings
It stirred the fragrant air
And called his name
Across the embered night.

He heard the promise
Troubled and with fear
And sought to override
Agnostic thought.
Who would believe a vision of this kind,
Of Messianic hope and Advent time?

Now mute
With trembling hands upon the latch
He glances back as if to catch his voice
Then turns to force ajar the heavy door
To stare into the faces by the gate
What faith alone perceives
And faith communicates.

Zebedee

I am the father of James and John,
I am their father—Zebedee.
'T was I the left in the boat alone
When they left their nets and the open sea.

"My sons, O my sons, my sons!" cried I.
"You belong to the wind and the sea."
But neither a lad turned back to speak
When they left their nets and the open sea.

For many a year I have fished these banks
Where my sons walked out of the sea.
But I've never hauled a teeming net
Since we fished together the open sea.

Now John was banished to die alone,
And James fell beneath Herod's sword.
But could Mary's lad have done it alone
Had the fisherman's sons remained at home?

Peter

Peter, I see thee,
Now the dawn is lighting.
Oh, that thou hadst not betrayed thy Lord!

He knows thy suffering
And thy faith-doubt anguish.
Yet he will climb Golgotha for thee.

Come, weep, dear Peter.
Weep for thy salvation.
Weep for thy Savior beneath his tree.

Auspicious Dreams

The Dalai Lama came to me one night
Appearing in the fragment of a dream.
I recognized his glasses and round face
And warm Tibetan smile filled with peace.
"How may I be of help?" he seemed to ask.
"I seek the truth," I whispered in his ear.

"And all that is both beautiful and dear."
He held his arms out wide, invitingly,
"Receive them," he replied, salvificly.
And in that instant just before I woke
I felt the presence of infinity
Grasp me in its calm eternity
And knew the Buddha as a treasured form
And norm of God's own grace and deity.

My mind recoiled with a modest start.
But my heart could not deny the power
Nor the bliss of that auspicious hour.

Table Talk

Somewhere between debut and final act
This play should grant an interlude.
If so, I would accept; nor would I quarrel or object.
I would recess; moreover I could do
With new rehearsals and could benefit
From revisions to the script.
It is no compliment to ad-lib one's farewell text.
In short, I would not mind
The curtain falling on this set.
But I am far upstage
And God the Father never yet
Has accepted second best.
Forgive if I digress
Seeing my own face in the chalice.

Something More

Sometimes I think I am a mystic,
Although I do not know what proposition
Best defines this disposition
Or what a mystic's task should be
In the final quarter of this century.

But "mystic" is, at least, an appellation
Which sometimes fits my cogitation,
My ups-and-downs and something more.

And, of course, it is this "something more" that
The metaphor in question begs to explore.
Augustine said it best long ago.
"I wish to know but God and the soul."

And that is proffered,
Never as a substitute for love of life or thought,
Nor as some antiquarian vision
Or saintly narrow cold aversion.

No. It is offered as a goal,
The Alpha and Omega of our hiddenness
Of the self's perpetual dialogue with its soul.

Faustus

Motivated by malevolent will
Faustus auditioned for the roll
It being his meontic hope
To vivisect his own ego
And if by some dark chance emerge
Co-equal with the Demiurge.
Down god-aisles he vainly strode
Impressed with Hell's rubric and verse
Quoting Mephistopheles
And praying to Lord Lucifer.

In the Shadowglen

In the Shadowglen

A catamount I dreamed last night stalked me in the woods.
Its paws were white and coat fawnlike and eyes a deep pool green.
I was surprised to realize the quiet cat's intent
And with reluctance bent a sapling quickly to the ground
And fashioned from its sweet gum rod a spear-like instrument.
I walked alone the forest path, watchful, wary, awed,
And as the wistful dream evolved, glanced backward
Shoulder-high to see the silent catamount wispily dissolve.
Now morning's light stirs drawn and pale,
The sky a dawn gray-blue. The stillness of the woods I love
Leads path-ward toward lush vines and gourds
Of purple black and dangling cords of wild muscadine.
And somewhere in the shadowglen of wildwood
Dreams and sleep, the restless catamount still stalks
The wooded tracts I love to walk and trails I guard and keep.

Doves

Sienna wings in swift seraphic flight
Bring silhouettes of gray to silver light
And banking in soft blurs above the millet
Descend in waves of brown to feed and billet
In the nearby woods. Such a perfect field!
How can they know its purpose is to yield
A harvest for the hunter in disguise?

The Owl the Deer and the Fox

I

Its icon eyes blinking
It watched me from its perch
Then spread its tattered feathers wide
To swoop across a broom-sedge sky
To rise again in search of prey
And glide into the cover of the pines.
So grand and ominous a fowl
Its life dependent on other life!
I felt embarrassed to avow
That mine is scarcely different.

II

Darting motion of tawny tan and agile form
Slipping between privet shoots and forest vine
Then bounding up one flash of final white
To disappear in twilight and gray pine.
Why am I startled?
Why the tom-tom primordial urge
To gawk and point and follow?

III

Lean shank of ruddy fur,
Rouge cousin of the canine,
I watch you loping through the mist
Of morning through our hamlet's groves
Of pecans as you slow your cant
Returning from your nocturnal throes.
Sly stalker of the neighborhood
You will not be domesticated.

Why am I not surprised or pleased
To watch you tiptoe by the trees
That border lawns and tall cornfields?
As the morning wears away
My heart lopes somewhere with you.

The Evening Call of Katydids

The evening call of katydids
Is a sharp staccato sound,
When a star-bright sky and darksome woods
Everywhere abound.

And the glowing night
Against that light
In the humid summer heat
Forms ineffably a mystery,

Measureless and profound,
And as far across as eternity
Bends heaven to the ground.

Summer in the Mountains

Roanoke

The early sun's bright rising rays
Fill the tree line with sparkling blaze
While high above the morning sky
Glows with soft translucence.

Frail gray quilts of dawn's thin haze
Blur the mountain orchards
Where bales of sage-green mellow hay
Hug the quiet meadows.

And silvery droplets of shimmering dew
Bathe tall stalks of bluets
And breezes stir with gentle keep
The last cobwebs of drowse and sleep.

To the Patter of Rain

Gray mist en-locks fog-veiled fields
Of blackened cornstalks bent and bowed
Swathed in drizzle and tattered cloud.

Dark, soft, earth-brown reds of autumn
Tint dogwoods and dapple pine
Draping gullies, ravines, and lanes
With broken bramble and kudzu vine.

And in the evening to the patter of rain
You come to me in the memory
Of a dress that rustled.

Connemara in the Fall

The bronze canopy catches the light
And sends it splintered
Through polished prisms of burnished red
And umber night.

The sound of oak leaves clacks
Throughout the forest,
Plates sifting down
Past crevices of hickory bark.

Leaves adrift and curled in sails
Tack the mountain pond
Encompassed by the silence
Drenched in endless sun.

And subtle tints of autumn hues
Diffuse pale patterns across felled logs
And crumbling edges of mossy bogs
Embroider borders of soft silk sedges.

While somewhere from his temple hidden
The last cricket of the dawn
Offers up his throbbing *matin*
And his farewell summer song.

Mirrorless Water

Bulldozer logged-scraped tracts of land
Leave dark red paths of mud behind
Brightened by the pink anomaly
      Of a redbud caught in yellow sand.

Along eroded fence banks grow
Velvet swaths of white-green moss
Edging termite puckered poles
      Near strands of red-leaf tangle briar.

And in the distance rise pine ridges
Black against a pale gray sky
While fishermen cast for largemouth bass
      In the inlet's vast and mirrorless water.

On Christmas Day

On Christmas day the blue birds came
And drank from puddles in the lane
While firecrackers everywhere
Filled the air with festive sound.

Evening

Shimmering saffron blazing globe
Hovering in an evening haze
Over wispy tall treetops
Interlocked in endless waves
Blotting out the lamplight's gaze
While westward pales the dusty disc
Dragging down night's long dark shade
With streaks of red in gentle rays.

Come Let's Go to the Lake and Sail

For Frank Handal

Come, let's go to the lake and sail
Now that our coves and creeks flow fallow.
Let's drive o'er to the lake and sail
To renew our hearts for a while.

For felled are the forests of fir
That our path-finding forebears knew
With only a murmuring wind
The soul to reassure.

The calm of the lapping wave
The wings of the swallow's flight
To cleanse the cluttered life
In the wake of rudder and sail.

So, to the waves we are bound.
Cleat off the sheets for a while
That the sailboat's silent pulse
May becalm our own somehow.

To the West Shines Venus

To the west shines Venus
In the evening sky
Low and comely
Where the twilight dies.

To the east-southeast
O'er a woods pine dense
Rides a moon-bright Jupiter
In full fulgence.

A rouge-dusk sun has sunk and set
While distant fires of a milky net
Blink white against a soft onyx
Of lamp-black night.

And I for an instant
Feel at one
With Jupiter, Venus,
And vanquished sun.

Our orbital planes
And concentric paths
But the finite rings
Of an infinite theme

Sailed out past the solar disc
To skip across our galaxy
Careening toward eternity
Carrying the heart's cry with it.

Connemara at Dawn

Purple petals etched on floating pads
Bob motionless upon the mountain mirror
Reflecting pine, rippling broken linden lines.

Glistening webs guard hemlock trails
And hike-worn shallow paths
Beyond the white and yellow flower
Beyond the oak and silent ash
Aglow in trellises of fire.

And buckeye acorns clutter winding climbs
Where mineral streams of smoke and rose
Stain the marbled forest floor

Along the ridge of rock and fern
Caped in fog and laurel berm
Iridescent in the pine.

Winter Mist

The mist with somber stillness
Pervades the winter wood
Where cedars in the distance
Bow cloaked in hazy hood.

Tree trunk and blackened plum limb
Blur in pale dimension
While fog swells drifting everywhere
Leave thin whispers in the air.

The First Frost of Autumn

The mantled kudzu mangled lies
Below bright mustard slopes
      Of golden rod

Where limpid claret sumac stems
And broken canes of cattails bend
      Among the dry milk pod.

I take the lane beside the brook
Below the granite crag
To stare into transparent pools
      Of blackened pebbled bark.

I lift my eyes to filtered light
By trickling droplets and gossamer falls
That slip across the worn dark ledges
      And down the quiet face of God.

And all scquestered in the jade
Of pine and laurel
I tread the root-webbed path
      Between the garnet beads of dogwood

Beneath the maple's scarlet brow
And sorrel petals of the ash.

Where All Things Go

I have seen the sourwood leaf
      Somersault silently to earth.
I have watched the winter mist
      Dust the oak of ancient girth.
I have felt the sting of wind
      Drive rain and blow with snow.
And passed a pair of junco
      Huddled hungry in the cold.

Winters come and winters go
      And dogwoods flower once again.
As wet magnolias blossom white
      In Leo's torpid days
Dragging dusty August down
      Into summer's restless night.

Return to Connemara

I come again to Connemara
>> To climb the woodchip path
>> Up between white pine and laurel
>> Past the hemlock, oak, and ash.

Subdued hues in mountain fog
>> Engauze broken pine boughs
>> The refuse of winter's rage
>> The ravages of icy claws.

I pause beside wide gnarled roots
>> And rough suede sod of carpet moss
>> And lichen dappled sheets of rock
>> To hear the patter of a falls.

In time I come to Glassy's peak
>> To quartz-white swaths of rippled stone
>> To solitude and solemn forest
>> Hushed in cloud and misty dome.

And the granite bald in the gray opaque
>> Extends to the distant pines
>> Where bay of hound and caw of crow
>> Drift upward from a road below.

And sodden oak leaves
>> Choke descending paths
>> Where hanging moss grows
>> O'er dogwood crags.

And lacquered ponds
>> Of dead pine needles
>> Ebb across the rock,
>> And oval cones

Like weathered bones
> Shed rain beads caught
> In crystalline drops
> Of pinpoints on pine tags.

I stop and listen to the silence
> Of ancient long and quiet centuries
> Visited here by owl and deer
> And roaming man in tribal band

All come to venerate the spirit
> Of Connemara
> Crowned in cloud
> And to renew their inner marrow.

Orion

To a Gull

Ah, solitary bird of sea and shore.
Like me you've come to greet the rising orb,
As manna washes in to feed your soul.
In my case, it's the Infinite within.

Your tripod toes, though awkward, serve you well,
Your eyes affixed on each incoming swell
Of foaming surf and sea green ocean shell.

Your Stoic posture in the silent sand
Reminds me of life's tested reprimand:
Whate'er befall, be stalwart, patient, true.

Lost virtues in our narcissistic day
Of Lincoln's "better angels" in dismay.

Heidegger

Dwelling's such a task while still alive.
It's only as we glance toward life's demise
That most of us realize its fabled prize
And wish we had lived better in hindsight
To cherish every hour of *Sein und Zeit*.

The Inner Oracle

We cannot force our Muse to speak her mind.
She has to come to us on her own time.
Otherwise, we compromise her voice,
Her Delphic verve that sounds the soul's remorse.

On Reading Yarmolinsky's Russian Poets

One's sore bestead to read a Russian's verse
So fecund with its love for Motherland—
However lyrical, however terse.
And underneath its sweep of all that's grand
Swells the poet's sorrow for the serfs,
Their sufferings and their lashes from their birth
Until emancipation set them free
In 1861
To suffer as poor peasants even more.
They write of numbing winters, bleeding sores,
Of lovers wrapped in fur as through the night
They marvel at the stars and Northern Lights,
Praying that their czars at last rescind
A poet's exile to Siberia's wind,
For writing rhymes exposing human woe.

The Young Housekeeper

Pisgah Inn

The morning sun had just begun to bathe
The quiet lodges with its burnished haze
Of dazzling gold and gleaming berry-pink,
Caught muted in long seams of velvet link.

Thus pleased to gaze upon dawn's fresh first light,
I was content to dwell upon the scene,
Until a young innkeeper came in sight
In blouse of sylvan green just to my right.

She too had come to view the vast ravine
Of coves encased in capes of autumn leaves.
Then leaning back against a huge green box,
—An AC unit built beside a rock—

She placed a plump red apple to her lips
And ate it slowly past her fingertips,
Into its yellow-white and mellow bowl,
While taking in the vista far below.

Her braided hair pulled back in ponytail,
I watched her from my room's recessed oak rail.
A long day lies before you, so I thought.
This morning's pause no doubt just one you've caught

To glance down slope before your mundane chores
Commence of changing sheets and sweeping floors.
So young; so many hopeful years to live,
So many morns to chase the life you'll give

Yourself and others, yet none like this,
For good or ill, ennobled by the sun.
You drop your eaten apple—seeds and core.
Your eyes diverted from the valley floor,

You turn and leave, as I lean out and watch
        you go.

I Dreamt I Rode a Unicorn

I dreamt I rode a unicorn,
A stallion white with spiraled horn,
Led by a virgin flaxen fair,
With sparkling starlight in her hair.

O, goddess sprite of purity,
Of comely grace and blessed beauty,
How aches my heart with penitence
That Time should send so innocent
A one as you to guide me through
Life's labyrinth of passing rue!
An exile lonely, long, intense
Of highest hopes, with best intent!

Starry Night

Robert Louis Stevenson

I hope to die on a starry night
Beneath its lambent glow,
Under its shining silent light
And wondrous star-white show,
As I cannot fathom a finer way
To say, "Farewell," and go.

Night

O dome of time's immortal glory,
Thou lighter of night's serenity,
Comfort my finite heart and story
With the calm of thy Eternity,
That all my faults and inner marrow
May find their mortal rest in thee.

Pilate's Courtyard

A brow without a nimbus for a crown,
Instead a wreath of nettled thorns pressed down;
Now scourged in Pilate's courtyard see him stand
Abandoned and despised by all on hand.

An Ecce Homo, gallant, dearest friend,
Who suffered on his cross to its sad end,
That we in suffering too might find a place
Within our hearts for kindness and for grace.

Orion

Hunter of the sylvan night
His canopy the stars
Orion strides beyond the light
Of Jupiter and Mars.

A marvel in his golden belt
Girdled round his lion's pelt
He bends in silence on his knees
With heart bowed toward the Pleiades.

O Seven Sisters to his West
He longs to hold you 'gainst his breast
With bow string taut upon his chest
Where will his Eros fall?

Good Morning, Sir!

For George Abernethy, January 1986

Hail, distinguished quiet man!
How your fine-trimmed moustache line
Befits your smile!

Your mannerisms have remained unchanged
And intellection burns as keen
As when you leaned across your desk
And taught us Plato's enduring quest,
Aristotle and Descartes,
Leibniz, Hume, Kant, and Sartre.

You took us journey inward from Plato's cave
Into the searing sun of all your questions,
Down ancient paths of intricate inspection
Of values and epistemology,
Through Nietzsche's thundering gorge,
Up toward Whitehead and something more.
You metaphysician!

Now you come to hear me speak
And still unnerve me
As I rustle the edges of my translations
Rendered from the Gallic tongue,
For presentation at this Colloquium.

"How can a philosophe like you keep silent?"
I tease you as you once teased me.
And you smile in reply, "It's easy."
And I am in the power of your spell again,
You grand Olympian and Socrates
Of my Athenian years at Davidson.

Lo, dear gray-haired mentor friend,
Whenever I am drawn to Plato's forms—
Those perfect patterns of truth and good—
My thoughts return to you.

Seneca's Advice

To learn how to live,
And to learn how to die,
Is the secret and essence of life.

There's a season for each,
And neither lasts long,
Whether filled with glory or strife.

A Dying Drunk's Confession

Three women I loved dearly,
Three women I did adore.
Two were angels from heaven,
The third a slut and a whore.

'T Was a Cool Morn

'T was a cool morn, with a windy breeze,
The stars only lightly aglow,
As I wandered out in the predawn night
Their glorious light to behold.

So shimmering pale each star appeared,
Alone in the sky's vast cold,
I couldn't help but wonder when,
As our galaxy grows old,
Their glow will thin as each star dims
In the sea of a huge black hole.

That day will come in a billion years,
Or a billion, billion more,
When the stars we love with wondrous joy
Burn out to shine no more.
And we who traced them through the night
Have long since gone before.

Aurelia

1935

A child born in a savage land
Beyond a crystal sea
Where a savage girl
With soft brown skin
Caressed and cared for me.

I hold her photo now in hand,
A sacred memory,
Of bamboo aisles
In that savage land
By the Filipino Sea.

Fitzgerald's *Rubaiyat*

His effervescent cup is O so real.
No hiding or pretending it is not.
Its immediacy refuses to conceal
That fleeting longed for joy in every heart.
'Till pompous conscience rears its pious thought,
And scolding brings love's fancy flights to naught.

Thoughts of Thanatos

Why do most thoughts of Thanatos
Cloak the heart with sorrow,
Since each of us must run life's race
In face of fate's tomorrow?
And sadly once all progeny we knew and loved are gone
We slip into that vacant space of empty cold beyond?
And where our eyes once smiled and gazed
From tinted frame
That too shall perish in the lake of devolution's flame?

My Neighbor's Jonquils

My neighbors' jonquils bloomed two weeks ago.
Mine, still in sheathes, have yet to show.
In time they will debut as weather warms
In stalks of green and yellow blossom swarms.

They don't last long, *you know*, three weeks at best,
Then brown and die to lie on Earth's sweet breast.
Say what you may, but spring without their presence
Would leave the landscape bare, shorn of their essence.

If Only You Were Here

A sunrise gray, through mist and haze
Summons the quiet viewer
To ruminate on other days
Of mist, and fog, and river.

Of lamplights dim along the James,
The nickel ribbon of the Seine,
Lapping past Lord Charlemagne,
Beside the gates of Heaven.

A child lonely by a brook,
A pensive student's overlook,
Two lovers on the river's brink
Reflected in the purple ink
Of Paris' wine and leaven.

A Wintry Wind

A wintry wind blew in with light snowfall,
Dusting pine boughs white beneath its pall.
Tonight its melting tufts will morph to ice
Until the morning sun can rise and slice

Seraphic dawn with rays of paradise,
Too bright and blinding for the eye to see
Beyond its glowing bowl and gleaming sea
The lodestar of our own longevity.

Grace

It would be nice if God might re-descend
To re-affirm the Savior he once sent.
But since we mocked and crucified the first
Why should he want a second to be cursed?
Unless he knew how brazen lost we are
To stretch his arms out once again so far?

Spes Alit Agricolam

I doubt my uncles ever knew the phrase:
Spes alit agricolam.
But more than once they'd oft allude
That "hope sustains the farmer."
Otherwise why did each Spring
They plow the clay red soil
Unless they hoped the Earth might bring
Their barely seed to flower?

A Rural Wedding

It's sad to be the officiant
In a wedding where no one is known
Where the bride stands beside the groom
In a silence all her own
Her eyes cast down
And his? God only knows!
And raising your hand to bless them
While waiting for them to kiss
All he does is stare at you,
Eager to be dismissed.

Art and Verse

Art and Verse

A picture's worth a thousand words they say
Until your heart collapses in life's fray
And longs for more than paintings on a wall
To bind your wounds and lift you from your fall.

That's not to claim that in some dire hour,
That art's without its own redemptive power,
As captured in Rembrandt's Bathsheba's eyes
While holding in her hand King David's verse:

"Now that I've seen you in the evening light
Your presence, love, I ask of you tonight.
My palace halls—perfumed in every suite—
Await the happy moment we shall meet.

"And on my part I shall do everything
To grant whatever wish that you might bring.
So, come, and quell my cup of loneliness,
With your sweet presence and your loveliness."

Which caused the tearful married girl to pause
And what the painter, Rembrandt, deftly caught,
As she glanced past her maid in shadowed-gauze,
Distraught by her own troubled, trembling heart.

An Unanticipated Call

She called, her voice close to the breaking point
And in between her sobbing gasps, he grasped:
An upstairs sink had overflowed and
Water now was pouring everywhere,
Seeping slowly through the bathroom's tiled cracks,
And running 'long the kitchen's ceiling's joints,
Had filled the kitchen floor with dripping junk.

"Ah, Love, I'm on my way to help!
Don't worry about the sagging ceiling joints,
The microwave or water on the floor.
All these we can clean up, or soon repair.
The one thing, though, I can't replace,
Is the precious girl I married and still love."

Hegel

Time's pendulum swings back and forth,
Bringing in both weal and woe,
And what one generation loves,
Its following will soon depose.

The Bell

I've had my share of dreams, its seems,
    Though each quite striking in degree,
But this one took me past a stream
    Above a valley floor,
And up a path and narrow lane
    I'd never walked before.
And mounted on a weathered pole
    A bell with tethered cord
Was hanging there for me to ring
    And listen to its toll.
And somewhere from the depths within,
    Within that silent space,
Came forth a quiet whispered voice:
    "Go on. Reach out and pull!
And when you pass this way again,
    Ring the bell once more."
And so I puzzle still this dream
    And all that it portends
That leaving what I've left behind
    All that I must transcend,
And in the end when coming home,
    May ring the bell once more.

Ruminations at the Beach

I have come to the balcony's window
To look outward from within,
So much has come to pass,
So much longs to ascend.

If I could draw a line,
Where should the chart begin?
With memories of the farm
Or eyes fixed on the end?

The past is past; the future still to be.
Why not enjoy the present calm
The stormy waves, their crashing balm,
As they wash back to sea?

Incoming Tide

Come walk with me along the beach
To gather shells within our reach,
Those fragile coral plates cast off
That once protected in their grip
The tiny lives the sea's stripped off.
      The tide is rising fast.
The morning's lamp shines through its golden glass,
Above the darkened clouds below;
Its steaming rays on sand alight,
Transforming surf in ribbons white
To flow across our ankles, wet and cold.

So Restful Falls the Snow

So restful falls the snow that fills the air.
Each tumbling flake so soft and crystal fair,
Descending down the steps of winter's stairs
To cloak the laurel leaves beside the gate.

And so each layer adds its lambent state,
In quiet moments white and all so rare,
Coming none too soon or none too late
To calm the harried heart of human plight.

So on they fall, in somersaulting flight,
Landing on their spread-out weeping wings,
To hush the restless rush of everything
And usher in the glow of limpid night.

In My Lover's Flowerbed

Above the low dark scattered clouds
Streams of contrails feather thin
Into the high cold stratosphere
Of clear blue sky and jet-stream wind.

While in my lover's flowerbed
Magnolia blossoms *font comme ça,*
In moon-white skirts with yellow hems.
The dying ones droop leather brown

To drop unnoticed to the ground,
To perish in green ivy vines
Tiered about a Buddha shrine
And purple iris dipped in wine.

Of Lately Now

Was lately now that I began
To read Ms. Dickinson again.
I found her cadence flowing free
Uncontrived, quite naturally,
Not always ending with a rhyme.
Most not more than twelve short lines.
Still a pleasant grace to hear
Her singing birds and humming bees.

She loved it all, small towns and fields,
Her solitude and neighboring hills,
Blessed with the whispers of her Muse
Who summoned all her wits to write
In praise of life howe'er she might.

She liked the phrase "divine intoxication,"
Which Orpheus and Dionysus would have approved,
As all three drank of the same brew.

My Native Drum

I have a native tom-tom, made by a Navajo,
Emblazoned with a raven bird, stretched on a hide of rose.
Five feathers to each wing, with stark and twisted claw,
Five feathers on its tail—fifteen all in all.

Five is the sacred sign of sun and corn and rain;
A fourth for snow and ice; the fifth where spirits reign.
Some say the numbers symbolize the tribes' ancient colors
Ranging from white to blue, then to bright corn-yellow,

And finally back to black, with red for war and trouble,
As one moves from the rising sun in cycles to cold winter—
A natural sphere and still revered high and holy order,
As venerable as Christ's five wounds and Moses' scrolls of Torah.

The Owl of Minerva

The owl of Minerva takes its solemn flight
But only at dusk and the gathering of night.
Hegel liked the thought of the bird as it soared
Over history's past, if such could be explored,
Provided its glide opened wisdom's door
For mankind to grasp the stubborn secret facts
That logic, art, and Right, and metaphysics track.

The Prize

I've come to prize the girl I love
Though prize was never the reason or cause.
'T was something in her smile and flair,
The sunlight in her auburn hair,
The way she turned and smiled at me
As if she too had found a prize.

The Poet

He left a string of poetry
Across the strands of time
Each meant to be mulled quietly
Though none was e'er sublime.

He simply wrote them as they came
In silent whisper and refrain
In rhythm with the universe
That sang to him in rhyme and verse.

A Prayer for Memorial Day

Eternal God of land and sea
Of sky and marsh, mountain and reef,
On this proud day we bend our knee
In gratitude for youth's belief
That service to our nation's call
Still deserves our all in all.
And we who love this cherished land
Ask Thee, O God, with them to stand
Upheld by thine own wounded hands
For all who love sweet Liberty.

Venus

Venus rising in the East
Brightest star of heaven,
Goddess of desire and love
Mother of Aeneas;
Queen of all, thou bride of dreams,
Dazzling in thy grandeur
Mortals of each passing year
Marvel at thy splendor.
Faces lifted toward thy light
Glow with Jove's own luster,
Each inspired to shine as bright,
Though stars of lesser glory,
All reflecting Rome's great might
And Romulus's story.

Remembrance

The silhouette of a bird
And the song of its call
Greet the rising sun
Peeking through silver fog.

From the height of its perch
In a Bartlett pear tree
Its song rings out
With a clear melody.

And nestled in leaves
Where its mate guards a nest
The sun softly falls on its
Bright scarlet vest.

And I see it's a finch
With its head cocked awry
Just as it takes flight
To slip off in the sky.

And the feeling of gloom
I have heretofore borne
Sails off on its wings
On that bright sunny morn.

Morning Silence

For all the bounteous wealth of nature
      Its beauty and array,
Its chanting birds and purple showers
      And goldfinch on display,
Its zinnias of myriad bloom
      Of orange and pink and beige,
The sad truth is you'll find a snake
      With semi-swollen flanks a-slake
Of speckled eggs it stole away
      From a finch's cradle chest,
Swaying in a hanging fern,
      Silent, empty, downy warm,
Amid a frantic feathered plaint
      Of lamentation in a song.

Nature

So fair and cruel can nature be,
An anomaly to its depth,
A food chain moving endlessly
From birth to sudden death.

The Dream

Last night's dream transported me on its wings to Paris,
Yet when I opened my billfold, no francs or Euros greeted me.
Nor for that matter airline stubs, nor departure times,
Nor how to find my way around Paris' metro lines.

Such a mental transportation, wrought with fear and hesitation,
Shocked me into wakefulness, accompanied with depression,
An emptiness within my heart for Paris' tree-lined boulevards,
Its Notre Dame and restful parks and café sanctuaries.

An Old Man's Morning

1

Been up since five a.m.
Sitting on the porch.
The moon still white and bright
So too the Morning Star.

Calm and cool right now
The sun will change all that
Gleaming in the East
In a saffron light.

2

How nice to see a star
In the morning sky
Knowing its been there
By the by-and-by.

To see it shining bright
Each morning I arise
Brings measure to my life
From Him who put it there.

The Rainbow

Against a drape of solemn black
Appeared the rainbow in the sky
Of purple, blue, yellow, and mauve
Until it faded in the glow
Of one last arc of pink sapphire,
All to the roll of thunder throes
Caught in webs of crinkling fire.

The Letter

He sat in stunned depression
The letter in his hand,
The agent wanted chapters,
Samples on demand.

He knew he had to send them
However great the cost
Of ceaseless consternation
Of talent being tossed.

And though his aspiration
Bubbled to the top
His road of broken hopefulness
Still numbed a broken heart.

He glanced across the meadow;
He glanced along its path,
At least the birds were singing
In dawn's bright aftermath.

Of Lips Last Kissed

Why must love's kisses end in tears?
Why can't it be quite other?
Why must across time's myriad years,
We can't forget the other?

The answer may be simple,
Though one the heart most fears.
For lovers' lips draw tenderness
From what is now and here.

We have so little time to drink
From a lover's cup of lips,
Let alone cling, lingering,
To the lips our own lips kiss.

And when those lips bid us farewell
And kiss before we part
How the memory of their spell
Taunts the empty heart!

Love's kisses seem to come with tears,
Especially in affairs,
Salty, wet, in furrows deep
And grandeur with despair.

We weep but though our faces dry
And cheeks return with color
The ecstasy of lips last kissed
Haunts on with each tomorrow.

There is a Beauty Beyond the Flesh

There is a beauty beyond the flesh
That only the heart can know.
There is a love that transcends time
That never can lose its glow.
There is a joy that none can steal
From hearts enjoined in love
Where stress nor sorrow nor tears that flow
Can diminish its hope or goal:
To be and remain one and the same
In the best of life and its flow
Where two hearts meet and find retreat
In the bonds of each other's soul.

The Idiopathic

Where has he gone, that consummate ethereal one?
Has he stolen away like Zarathustra, since his days are done?
Like Zeus, Apollo, Ra, and Jove across the sky's domain,
He too has waved "good-bye" to hosts
Whose priests he once ordained. From the glint in their eyes
To impatient sighs, he knew it was time to go,
To say "farewell" and then slip out
 And quietly close the door.

Life has no time for him right now; no Ultimate to adore.
Only the now consumes one's time, it and little more.
The day of Time's Immortals is irrelevant in our mind.
They had their holy hour, their devotees and shrines,
Their history and mythologies of sacred bread and wine.
Now it is only the urgent, the anxious that's divine,
Where chaos reigns and the insane exercise their power.
And time has lost all measure in the pit of human mire.
And the idiopathic puzzles us in all that we aspire.
And the Metaphor that once fed hearts
In turn we now devour. The way the Titans ate
Dionysus, and Cronus castrated his father.

The Pre-Dawn Sky

Come watch with me the pre-dawn sky
As God enrobed in stars slips by.
You'll find him just northeast of Mars
Beyond Orion's belt of stars
Or helping Venus shine with light
While bidding Jupiter "Good-night!"

The Total Eclipse

For months they traced its path
The arc that it would take
As sun and moon and earth
Aligned to take their place
Along its scenic route
Beneath its measured pace
As human eyes gazed on
That brief phenomenon
That only shielded eyes
May ever see.

Jakkov ben Yitzak

Fearful on the ground he lay
Impulsive and uncertain.
Hebron to his south now lay;
North, and unknown future.

Restless in his dream he tossed
Beneath the stars of heaven,
Portals of a holy night
Aglow with flights of angels

Descending and ascending
In silent voices singing.
And above a light so bright
Blinding his own vision.

Suddenly the ground grows hard
Rocks everywhere abounding.
"God is here," whispers the night,
"His grace forever sounding."

Humble in the dawn's new light
He builds a rock cathedral
A solitary stone to mark
Where God found him while fleeing.

We too have bouts of fear and doubt,
Impulsive and uncertain.
Yet on life's rocks of darkest night
God's angel stars draw near,

Descending and ascending
With love divine, all-mending.
And above that Light of Lights,
Transcending even angels.

If Only I Could Climb the Stars

For Alice Anne

If only I could climb the stars
And soar on wings like seraphim
What might I find, what might I see
As I slipped by each galaxy?

The glowing blue of nebulae
The purple clouds of distant skies
Of planets in bright orange sunset
Orbiting their solar stars

Drifting through vast sparkling nets
Of twinkling ions in lilac mists
Until on Twilight's edge of Time
I'd long for thee again.

Orion Unrequited

They placed him in a parabola
As eyes may easily see,
A geometric symmetry
Of angles and degrees.

What made the demiurge inclined
So to confine this star,
This constellation of brilliant light
In arcs of concave bars?

Some say it was the Pleiades
Who feared his magma fire
Lest his heart of lust and fame
Consume them in his ire.

And so they flee across the night
Each sister's lamp, dimmer,
While hieroglyphic in his cage
He stares out, unrequited.

Corona Moon

Seeping through night's silver sheen
      Glows the moon in silence
In starlight tantamount to see
      Its open staring iris
A finite regal platinum sphere
      Against infinity
A corona bright with rings of gold
      On bronze-tipped eyebrow wings
With its mystic eye affixed
      And staring down on me.

About the Author

Born in the Philippine Islands, Benjamin W. Farley was reared on tobacco and cattle farms around Abingdon, VA. He is a graduate of Davidson College (AB) and earned his master's degree and doctorate of philosophy from Union Theological Seminary in Richmond, VA. As an ordained minister, Farley served Presbyterian churches in Virginia from 1964-1973. Farley was Younts Professor of Philosophy and Religion at Erskine College, Due West, SC, where he taught from 1974-2000. During his tenure at Erskine, Farley was the recipient of the Excellence in Teaching Award three times. He is the author of eight scholarly works, two collections of meditations, two of short stories, and author of five novels, a sixth forthcoming. He currently resides in Columbia, SC with his wife, Alice Anne.

Books of related interest to readers of his poems would include *Three Thousand Days and Nights, Beyond Homer, Quilly Hall, By the Waters of Babylon*, and *Corbin's Rubi-Yacht.*